WOMAN
NO LONGER A LITTLE GIRL

DOROTHY A. COOPER

KATRINA'SWORKS
PUBLISHING LLC

No part of this book may be used or reproduced in any matter without permission, except in the case of brief quotations embodied in articles or reviews.

Models used for cover and trailer were acquired from canstockphoto.com

All rights are reserved by the author.

ISBN-13:978-0692864388

ISBN-10:0692864385

Woman

No Longer A Little Girl

DOROTHY A. COOPER

Copyright © March 2017

*Graphics supplied by the author

Katrinasworks.com

INTRODUCTION

It was such an honor to be invited to Terry's Event Center last year, by the West Memphis Area Alumnae Chapter of Delta Sigma Theta Sorority, Inc. Mrs. Tracey LaBattes Parker, President.
To go stand before "The Love Jones Experience" and share my thoughts on love through spoken words, as a published author, at the time of two books, left my heart overwhelmed and excited about it all.
The story shared was riveting, pulsating, and deep just as it was written to be. I was so thrilled to see and hear, also, how the verbiage of my inner most thoughts left all hearts captivated by its truthfulness told.
"A Conscious Black Man and His Black Skin", soon after the experience, became my third published book and also, so far, my best seller. Now, I am so thankful for the opportunity of being invited back for "The New Love Jones Experience". This time I ask that you sit back, relax, and enjoy the Spoken Words as they are read from my fourth book due to be out, March 2017. With no further ado, I shall continue the conversation surrounding the love of "A Conscious Black Man and His Black Skin" from the heart of "Woman No Longer A Little Girl"….

May every branch,
May every limb,
Upon this tree -
Represent the lineage
Of my Ancestry;
For without their existence,
There would be no me!

Dorothy A. Cooper

WOMAN NO LONGER A LITTLE GIRL

While sitting all alone

In the still of the darkness

In my living room

A few short nights ago,

It brought peace

To the mind

And a special joy

Deep down on the inside

To know I am

Woman

No longer a little girl!

Patiently awaiting the sizzling touch

Of a conscious Black Man

And his Black skin

As I am invited

To be a part of his world!

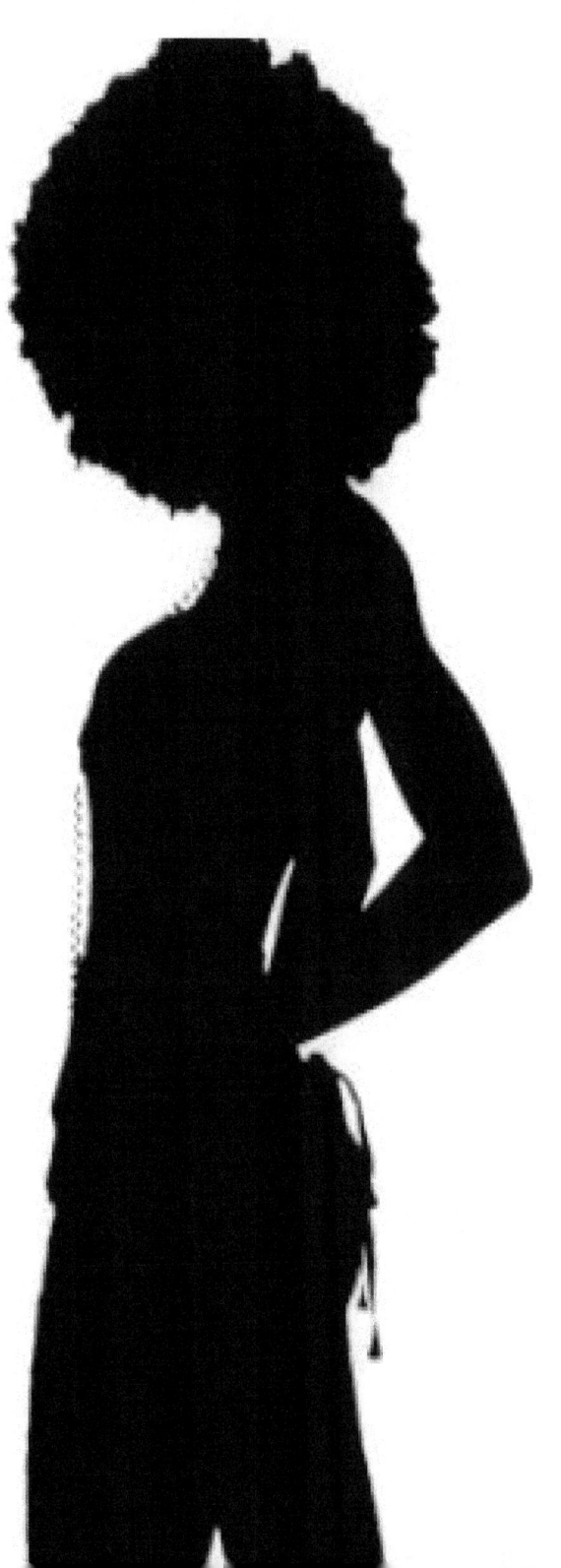

See as a Woman

No longer a little girl

I have come to learn

Down through the years

My needs

Mental, physical, sensual

Can only be fulfilled

By a compatible

Conscious Black man!

One with no reservations

In being everything

Woman,

No longer a little girl,

In a man, needs!

For she has no hesitation

In return

To make sure he,

For his goodness,

Is very well pleased!

A conscious Black man!

One who fully understands

The history of

His Black skin

Which was simply formed

By the blood

Of his forefathers hands!

In fact just to be able

To have a conversation

With him,

A conscious Black man,

That is,

There is no doubt

It will be intelligent and real,

For it is sure to take

Woman,

No longer a little girl,

Higher

And fill her every desire

With fire!

My! My! My!

It takes a

Woman,

No longer a little girl,

However,

To understand

It is disrespectful to

Harbor any doubts,

Or feelings to hurl

When hearing of

The Conscious Black man

And his Black skin

Was formed

To be

God of this world!

Oh Yes! It is true!

Specifically,

With the main purpose

Of being

The head and not the tail!

First and not last!

There are many History books

Out there

Which tells the truth of the past!

Hebrew Israelite,

Holiness' plight,

Nation of Islam, too,

Matter of fact

Even some Black

Christian men

Are conscious approved!

Conscious Black man

I, Woman

No longer a little girl

Adore you!

For

The thickness of the girth

Of your worth

Which is your manhood

From the deepest part

Of my soul's birth

Baby,

One thought of you

Makes my entire body

Feel

So, so, good!

Oh yes!

It's true!

Nonetheless,

Not every Black man

I must confess

Is conscious of the purpose of

His Black skin.

Certainly it is not

For using his hands

Every chance he gets

To destroy his brother

Mother, or sister, too!

Because of being mad

At a father

He never knew!

But loudly

To you I proclaim

Have no fear

Conscious Black man!

Instead

Pull up your pants!

Put down the gun

And the drugs

Then find comfort in the fact

Every day you wake up

On this side of heaven

And your skin is Black

Is an opportunity

To walk proudly in royalty!

Conscious Black Man!

Wake up!

However, for to keep

Playing the blame game

Is the reason

For results ending the same!

Locked up!

Dead!

In the grave!

You know it's true!

But don't you desire better

For your son, if not for you?

So he too

Won't get arrested

For doing something destined to leave his

soul numb!

Wake up! The choice is yours.

Then again,

Not every Woman

Understands,

The importance

Of the stance

Of a conscious Black man!

That is unless she is

Woman

No longer a little girl!

With the determination to be

Everything

A conscious Black man

Needs in this world!

Oh yes, you know

It is true!

But expectation

Should not be

For her to

Continuously

Do for you,

Unconscious Black man,

When negativity

Is the only answer

Your heart repeatedly

Keeps

Putting her through!

Wake up!

The choice is yours!

But through

It all,

From this day forward,

Man and Woman

Especially those with

Black skin

Must proudly be found

Lifting up one another

To higher grounds!

In our speech

Let us proclaim

The other by the names

Of King and Queen

Just as the Creator,

God Almighty,

Created us to be!

Indeed!

Then, suddenly,

As my thoughts preceded,

Slowly as I moved

From the couch

To the chair,

A vision came of how nice

It would be

If a conscious Black man

And his Black skin

Was waiting there!

To hold me in his arms

And fill all of my

Womanly charms

With longevity's thrust!

While my fingertips

Gently massaged his warmth,

Oh, it was

Such a beautiful thought!

Conscious Black man?

Don't you understand?

Being in your arms

To a Woman

No longer a little girl

Means

Safety, security,

And no worries

Of mastering any storm

Out to do her harm?

For she knows

She has you,

Conscious Black man

And your Black skin, too,

To motivate her

While pushing

Her through,

It all!

In fact,

It must be love!

For only love

Can hold love, sincerely

Then, leave love

In love, clearly

With love, immediately thereafter

And for a lifetime!

If it is love.

It is the only way!

Perhaps,

This is why I say

Conscious Black man

I'm already in love with you!

And I wait

So the love received in return

Will be true,

Mutual, powerful, desirable!

Yes, fire, and desire, baby!

In fact,

Only your key,

Conscious Black man

Was made to fit

The design of my hole,

Woman,

No longer a little girl,

Perfectly!

Think about it!

Think about it some more!

Indeed!

Oh, how my alter-ego,

Anne,

Is ready to fill

Every inch of her desires

With your fire

Conscious Black man

And your Black skin, too!

For Anne to be able

To take over

My jewel,

Which is my pearl,

And replace it

Back and forth

With her tongue's swirl,

Ummm…

My! My! My!

Is guaranteed every time,

To make you – come – over

Any fears, that is...

Of a Woman

No longer a little girl!

A Woman who is ready

To follow God's plans

Of being "a good thing!"

A Woman, one who understands,

The job of a Woman,

No longer a little girl,

Is to stick

Closer to you,

Then, that

Long big vein

Running along side

Of your hand.

And especially the vein,

You know the one

At your pinnacle point

Which protrudes out

On the side of your head!

Yes! Yes! Yes!

A woman,

No longer a little girl

Whose conversation

Is just as deep as yours!

With a voice

Unafraid

To speak the truth

Even to you

Conscious Black Man!

Ooohhhh!

Conscious Black man

As I shake my head

Back and forth,

How you exasperate me!

How just the thought of you

Sets my fluids

To running freely!

Like a fire

Burning hot with desire!

My! My! My!

Such a hard worker

You are too!

I, Woman

No longer a little girl,

Am learning so much

Just by being able

To watch you

From a distance! That is…

Staying focused!

Making no time for play!

On purpose!

No matter how many

Different size hips

May sway your way!

Conscious Black man,

However,

Strongly, to you I say,

I cannot learn my place

From no other man

Of any other race!

For Brother,

The only one

Who knows

What I, as a Black Woman,

No longer a little girl,

Have made it through,

Is you!

You are my example,

Conscious Black man!

So lead me, guide me,

Take me by my hand!

Show me the way

With your Black skin!

Do not push me to the side!

Let me in…

For, I need you to know

A Conscious Black Man

Was not meant to be alone!

It is too hard

For you to be out there,

Brother,

Laboring on your own!

A Woman

No longer a little girl

Is what you need.

Otherwise,

Your heart

Will remain unpleased!

So come

Let us built

A garden together

While standing nude

In the warm spring weather!

Let us make love

On the grounds

Of the fresh morning's dew

Then replenish our strength

From the juice

Which shall flow freely

From inside all things

Which surrounds us

Which are sweet

And good for the

Nourishment of our spirits!

Over and over again!

As our lips

Touch the very center of

The passion fruit's core!

Yes! Yes! Yes!

Take me!

I am yours!

Let us not stop,

Until we hear

The voice

Of Almighty God,

Himself!

As we let out Gasping sounds of joy

I, Woman,

Now know,

Conscious Black man,

You are my hero!

So, please

Forgive me

For any part,

Earlier on,

I played

In tearing up

Your heart.

Let me also mention

I am paying attention

For I have been

Transformed

To know

When you come!

For it certainly

Shall be

By the deepness

Of the sound beating

From the drum

Which shall be

My heart!

So now, here,

As I stand

Confident in

Who I am

Sincerely

I ask every Woman,

No longer a little girl,

Collectively,

Will you stand with me?

Please?

Now, respectively,

Out of love,

Let us together, resort

To raising our fist

High unto the sky

In support

Of every

Conscious Black Man

And his Black skin!

Conscious Black Man…

YOU ARE SO GREAT!

YOU ARE SO GREAT!

YOU ARE SO GREAT!

FROM

THE

HEART

OF

WOMAN

NO

LONGER

A

LITTLE

GIRL!!!

I SALUTE YOU!!!

DOROTHY A COOPER

AUTHOR

Ann Dyson, as the author prefers to be called, after experiencing the hardships associated with being homeless, never gave up on her faith. She believed in her heart God would give her *ANOTHER CHANCE* to serve Him, through Christ Jesus, the way He deserves to be served.

Connect with Dorothy
On
Facebook
https://www.facebook.com/DADysonCooper/

Katrinasworks.com

www.ingramcontent.com/pod-product-compliance
Lightning Source LLC
Chambersburg PA
CBHW051706090426
42736CB00013B/2561